Maths
made easy

Key Stage 1
ages 5-6
Advanced

Author
Sue Phillips

Consultant
Sean McArdle

D1439675

LONDON • NEW YORK • MUNICH • MELBOURNE • DELHI

Numbers

Write the numbers.

0 0 0 0

1 1 1 1

2 2 2 2

3 3 3 3

4 4 4 4

5 5 5 5

6 6 6 6

7 7 7 7

8 8 8 8

9 9 9 9

Continue the pattern.

1 5 7 1 5 7

3 6 9 3 6 9

2 4 8 2 4 8

Writing numbers

Count, write, and say the number of letters.

Christina 9 nine

Tarik

Grandad

Happy Birthday

Good Morning Everyone

How are you today?

Write your name.

Make up your own message.

Counting

Write the missing numbers.

Counting in 2s

Hop in 2s. Colour the squares

Elizabeth Even

Oliver Odd

0	1	2	3	4	5	6	7	8
17	16	15	14	13	12	11	10	9

0	1	2	3	4	5	6	7	8
17	16	15	14	13	12	11	10	9

What letters will you find? Say the numbers as you draw.

```
2   4   6   8       •
0   22  12  10      •
    20  14          •
    18  16      •   •
•   •   •   •
```

```
8 • 6 • 4 • 2 •     •
10• 32• 34• 0•      •
12• 30•     •   •
14• 28• 26• 24•     •
16• 18• 20• 22•     •
```

```
0 • 2 • 8 • 10•     •
30• 4 • 6 • 12•     •
28• 22• 20• 14•     •
26• 24• 18• 16•     •
•   •   •   •   •
```

```
16• 14•     •   •   •
18• 12•     •   •   •
20• 10•     •   •   •
22• 8 • 6 • 4 • 2 •
24• 26• 28• 30• 0
```

Write the numbers.

Even numbers

2   4   6   8   ☐   ☐   ☐   ☐   ☐   ☐

Odd numbers

1   3   5   ☐   ☐   ☐   ☐   ☐   ☐   ☐

Odd and even numbers

Colour the
even numbers.

1	7	3	19	13	5	21	9	15
5	3	2	4	12	8	4	23	17
9	15	10	15	3	11	4	19	9
25	5	2	21	15	1	20	13	7
5	17	24	6	18	4	14	17	3
23	13	2	3	7	19	16	23	7
3	5	10	25	1	7	12	21	3
5	7	6	18	22	10	6	17	5
1	5	3	9	17	21	19	5	3

24	4	6	18	14	22	10	8	2
2	6	3	9	17	21	19	2	4
4	8	13	2	4	12	8	4	6
18	4	3	12	22	18	14	6	24
20	10	1	7	3	19	13	6	2
6	18	12	10	14	6	1	8	12
10	14	22	12	14	20	5	14	12
12	18	23	5	21	17	19	22	18
14	8	16	4	12	6	10	22	16

Colour the
odd numbers.

Counting in 10s

0	10	20	30	40	50	60	70	80	90	100
zero	ten	twenty	thirty	forty	fifty	sixty	seventy	eighty	ninety	one hundred

How many sweets? Count, say, and write.

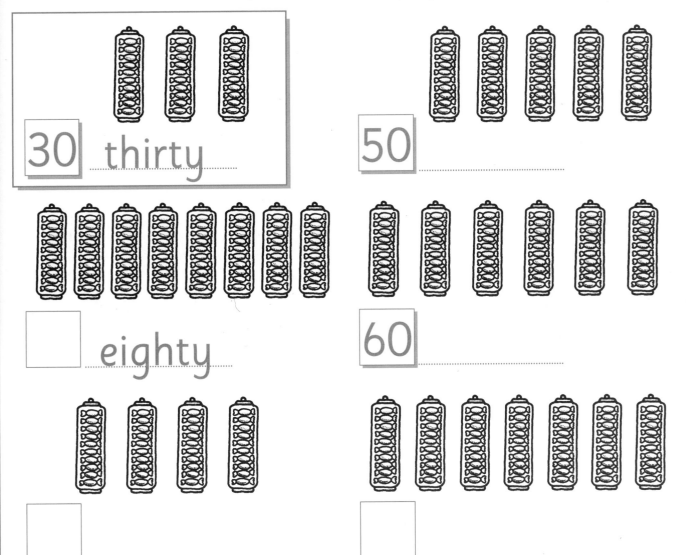

30 thirty

50 _____

_____ eighty

60 _____

_____

_____

Put the numbers in the right order

~~10~~ 60 100 50 ~~20~~ 70 90 30 40 80

10 20 ....

Biggest first

100 90 80 ....

7

Counting in 3s, 4s, and 5s

Draw pathways by writing the missing numbers.

Steps of 3

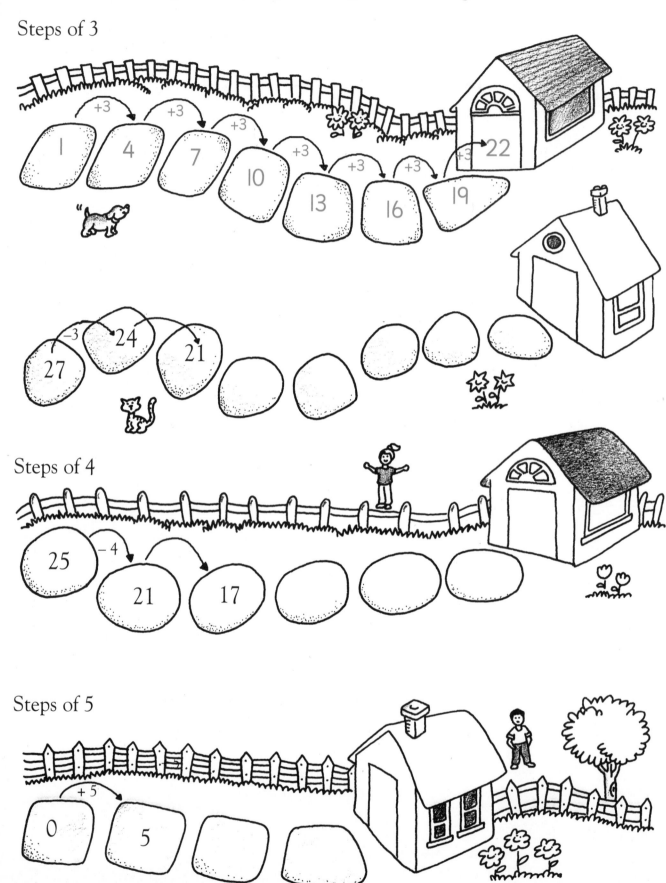

Steps of 4

Steps of 5

Reading numbers

Join the numbers and complete the drawings.

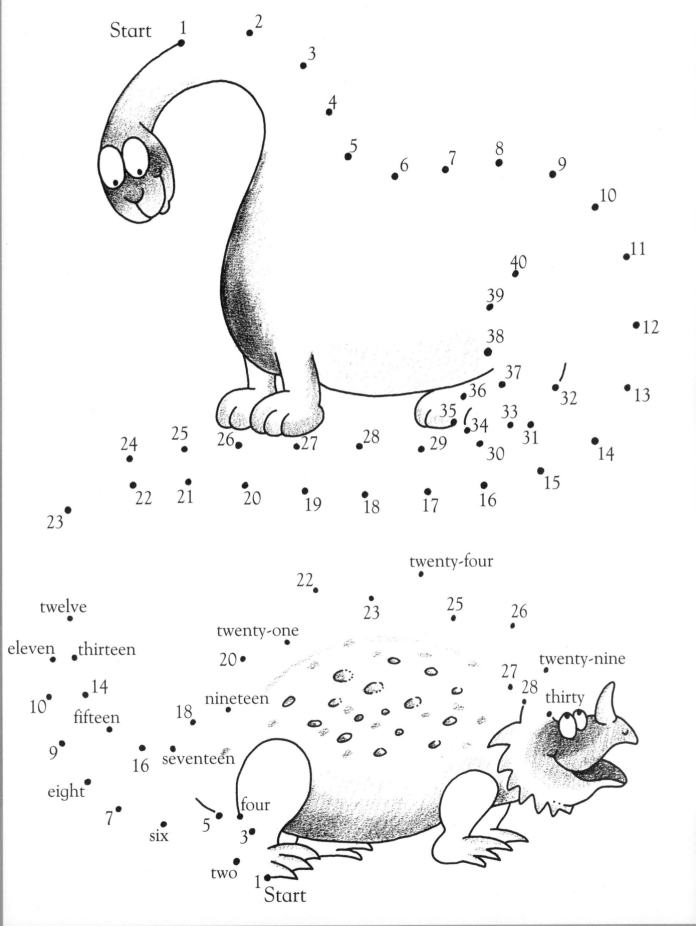

Start 1 2
3
4
5 6 7 8 9
10
11
40
39
12
38
37
36 32 13
35 33
34 31
30
29 15
24 25 26 27 28 16
22 21 20 19 18 17 16
23

twenty-four

22

twelve 23 25 26

eleven thirteen twenty-one twenty-nine
20 27 28 thirty
14 nineteen
10 fifteen 18
9 seventeen
eight 16
7 four
six 5
three 2
two 1 Start

Tens and units

Write the tens and units.

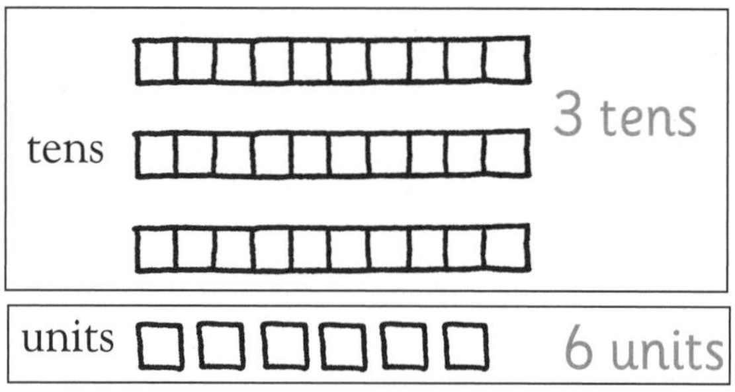

tens 3 tens

units 6 units

30

6

30 + 6 = 36

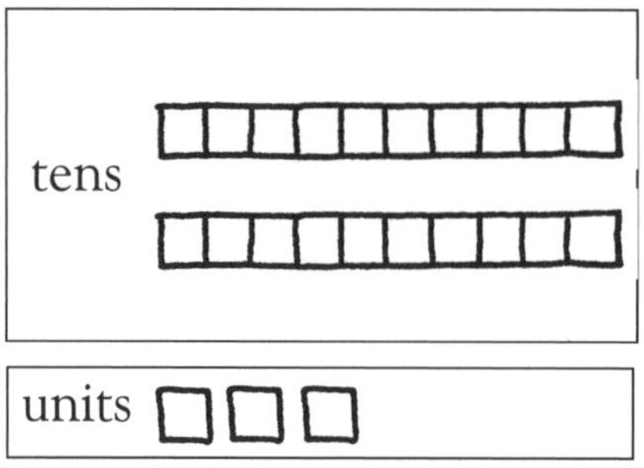

tens

units

☐

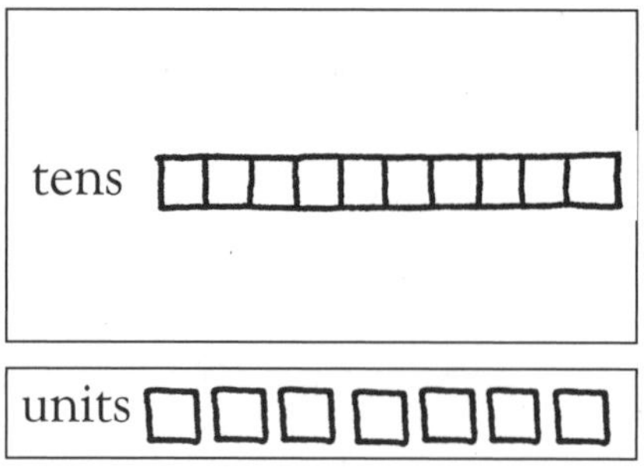

☐

+ =

tens

units

☐

☐

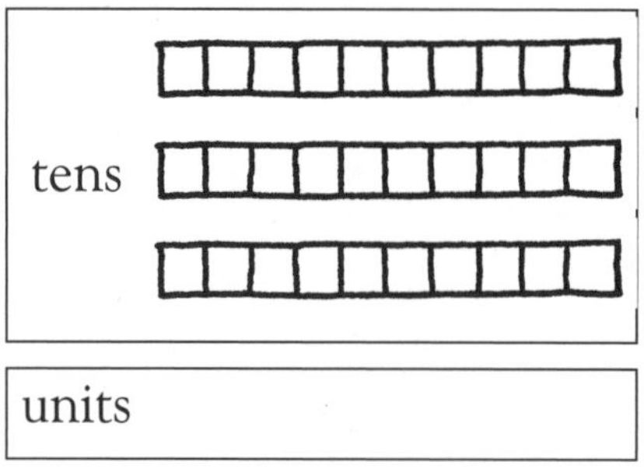

+ =

tens

units

☐

☐

+ =

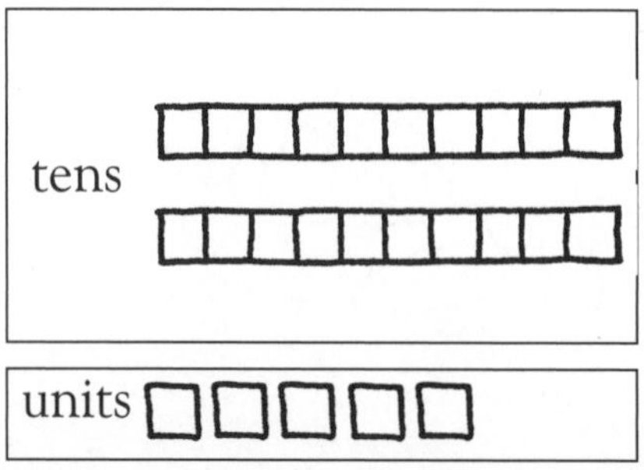

tens

units

☐

☐

+ =

Comparisons

Write more than or less than.

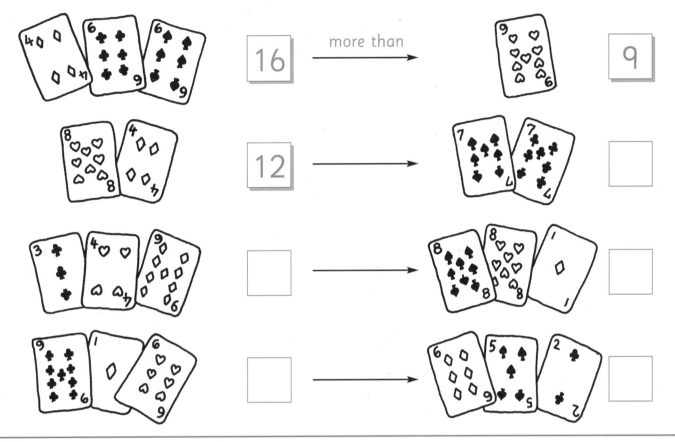

Write 1 more, 1 less, or in-between.

1 less	in-between	1 more
20	21	22

1 less		1 more
	26	

	in-between	
19		21

1 less		1 more
	29	

1 less		1 more
	11	

	in-between	
30		32

Comparing money

Colour the one who has the most money.

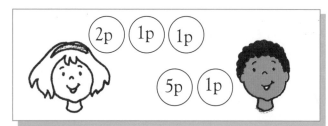

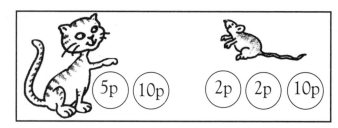

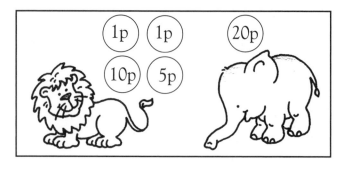

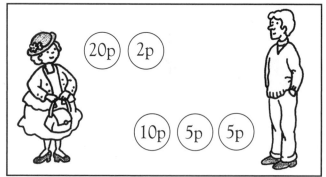

Draw some coins in the purses.

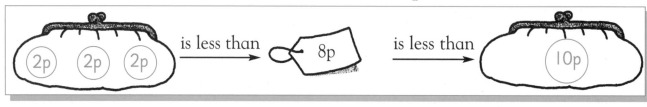

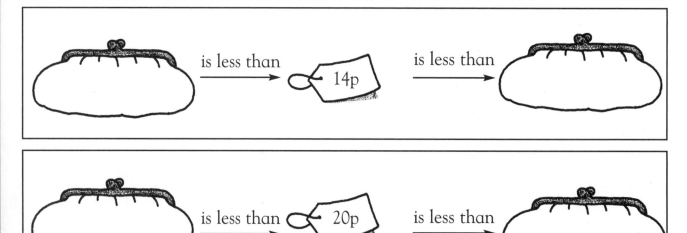

Spot the doubles

Draw the missing spots and write the numbers.

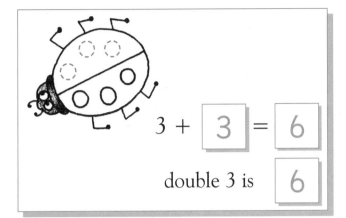

3 + 3 = 6

double 3 is 6

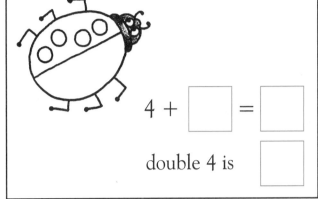

4 + ☐ = ☐

double 4 is ☐

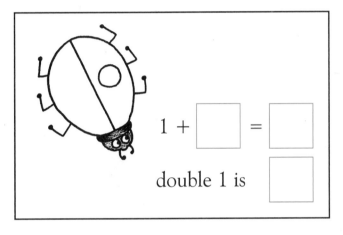

1 + ☐ = ☐

double 1 is ☐

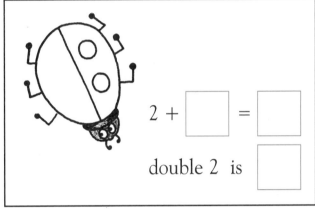

2 + ☐ = ☐

double 2 is ☐

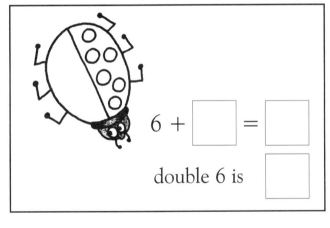

6 + ☐ = ☐

double 6 is ☐

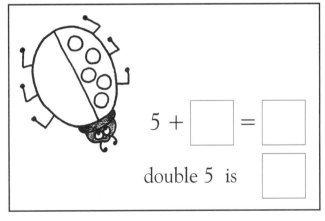

5 + ☐ = ☐

double 5 is ☐

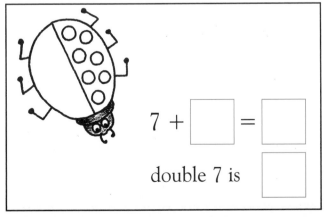

7 + ☐ = ☐

double 7 is ☐

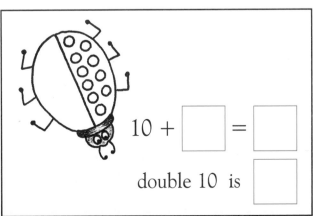

10 + ☐ = ☐

double 10 is ☐

10 more or less

Find 10 more than each number on the rocket.

Find 10 less than each number on the rocket.

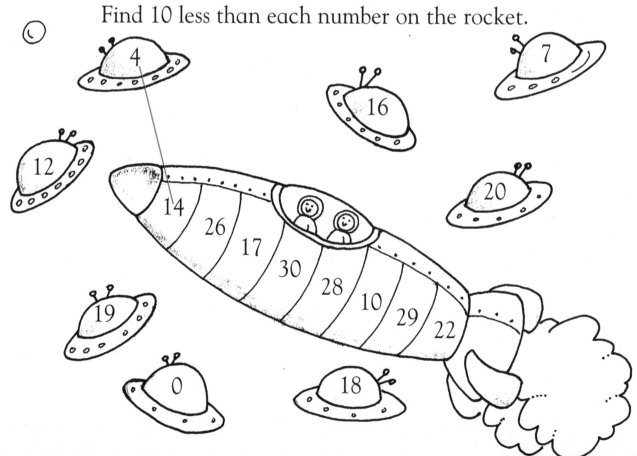

Ordinals

Colour the beads.

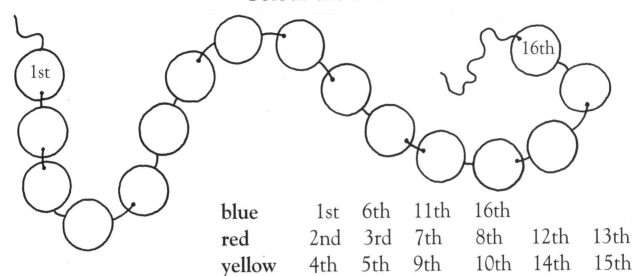

blue	1st	6th	11th	16th		
red	2nd	3rd	7th	8th	12th	13th
yellow	4th	5th	9th	10th	14th	15th

Write the positions.

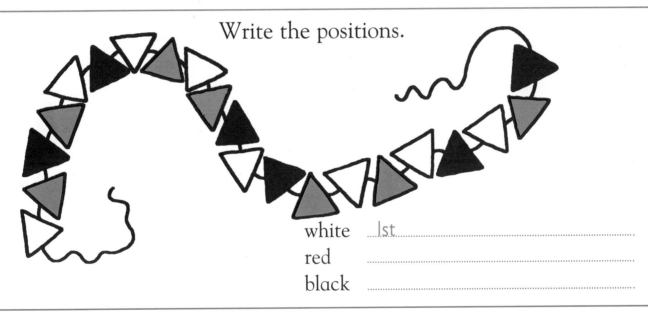

white _1st_ ....

red ....

black ....

Choose 3 colours. Make your own pattern. Write the positions.

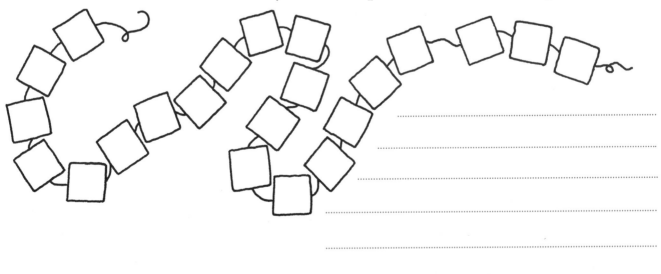

....

....

....

....

....

Ordering

Write the numbers in order.

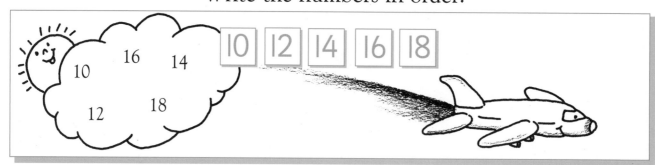

10	12	14	16	18

8	7	6	5	4	3

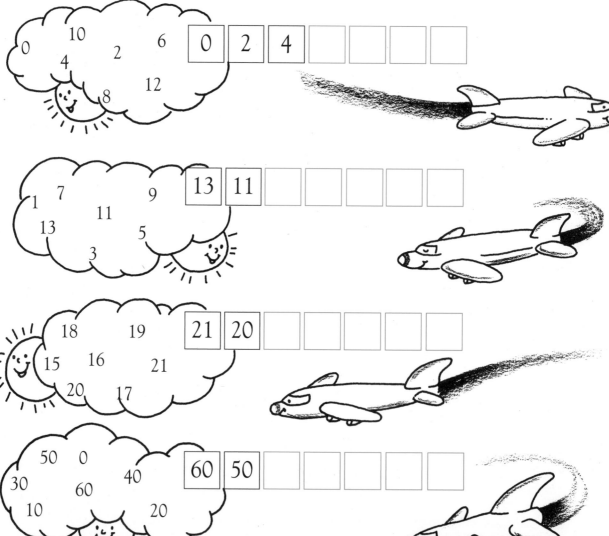

0	2	4				

13	11				

21	20				

60	50				

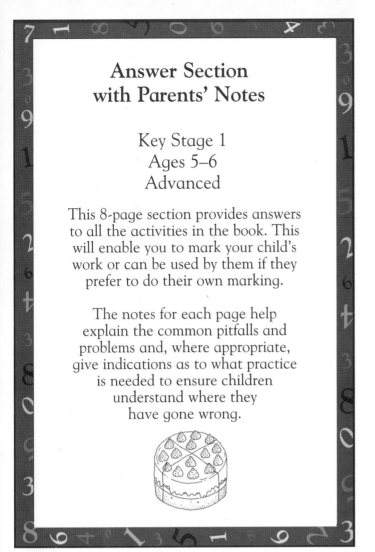
2 ⭐ ## Numbers

Write the numbers.

0 0 0 0 0 0 0 0 0 0 0 0 0 0
1 1 1 1 1 1 1 1 1 1 1 1 1 1
2 2 2 2 2 2 2 2 2 2 2 2 2 2
3 3 3 3 3 3 3 3 3 3 3 3 3 3
4 4 4 4 4 4 4 4 4 4 4 4 4 4
5 5 5 5 5 5 5 5 5 5 5 5 5 5
6 6 6 6 6 6 6 6 6 6 6 6 6 6
7 7 7 7 7 7 7 7 7 7 7 7 7 7
8 8 8 8 8 8 8 8 8 8 8 8 8 8
9 9 9 9 9 9 9 9 9 9 9 9 9 9

Continue the pattern.

1 5 7 1 5 7 1 5 7 1 5 7
3 6 9 3 6 9 3 6 9 3 6 9
2 4 8 2 4 8 2 4 8 2 4 8

Good number formation needs regular reinforcement at home. Poorly formed numbers quickly become a habit which only regular practice and checking can undo. It is important to watch the children as they write, making sure that all digits begin at the top.

3 ## Writing numbers ⭐

Count, write, and say the number of letters.

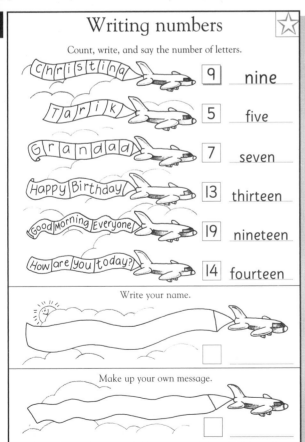

Christina — 9 nine
Tarik — 5 five
Grandad — 7 seven
Happy Birthday — 13 thirteen
Good Morning Everyone — 19 nineteen
How are you today? — 14 fourteen

Write your name.

Make up your own message.

Although the spellings of some of the numbers are complicated, children should now recognise letter patterns and use them to spell other words. 'Forteen' would be an attempt worth praising as the 'teen' section has been remembered and used.

4 ⭐ ## Counting

Write the missing numbers.

Some children may find it difficult to 'cross over' a ten, for instance 19 *20* 21. It will help to go back to 1 and to recite the numbers up to that point.

Counting in 2s

Hop in 2s. Colour the squares

Elizabeth Even

Oliver Odd

| 0 | 1 | 2 | 3 | 4 | 5 | 6 | 7 | 8 |
| 17 | 16 | 15 | 14 | 13 | 12 | 11 | 10 | 9 |

| 0 | 1 | 2 | 3 | 4 | 5 | 6 | 7 | 8 |
| 17 | 16 | 15 | 14 | 13 | 12 | 11 | 10 | 9 |

What letters will you find? Say the numbers as you draw.

Write the numbers.

Even numbers

2 4 6 |8| |10| |12| |14| |16| |18| |20|

Odd numbers

1 3 5 |7| |9| |11| |13| |15| |17| |19|

Can the children talk about the difference between Elizabeth Even's and Oliver Odd's hops? Tell them that counting in 2s is really like missing out a number every time. Encourage children to recite the sequences until they become automatic.

Odd and even numbers

Colour the even numbers.

1	7	3	19	13	5	21	9	15
5	3	2	4	12	8	4	23	17
9	15	10	15	3	11	4	19	9
25	5	2	21	15	1	20	13	7
5	17	24	6	18	4	14	17	3
23	13	2	3	7	19	16	23	7
3	5	10	25	1	7	12	21	3
5	7	6	18	22	10	6	17	5
1	5	3	9	17	21	19	5	3

Colour the odd numbers.

24	4	6	18	14	22	10	8	2
2	6	3	9	17	21	19	2	4
4	8	13	2	4	12	8	4	6
18	4	3	12	22	18	14	6	24
20	10	1	7	3	19	13	6	2
6	18	12	10	14	6	1	8	12
10	14	22	12	14	20	5	14	12
12	18	23	5	21	17	19	22	18
14	8	16	4	12	6	10	22	16

Here, children make a decision about whether the number is odd or even, when it is not in sequence. More work on the pattern of even 2s would be beneficial if your child finds this hard.

Counting in 10s

Use this number line to help you.

| 0 | 10 | 20 | 30 | 40 | 50 | 60 | 70 | 80 | 90 | 100 |
| zero | ten | twenty | thirty | forty | fifty | sixty | seventy | eighty | ninety | one hundred |

How many sweets? Count, say, and write.

|30| thirty |50| fifty

|80| eighty |60| sixty

|40| forty |70| seventy

Put the numbers in the right order.

~~10~~ ~~60~~ ~~100~~ ~~50~~ ~~20~~ ~~70~~ ~~90~~ ~~30~~ ~~40~~ ~~80~~

10 20 30 40 50 60 70 80 90 100

Biggest first

100 90 80 70 60 50 40 30 20 10

Check the spelling of 'forty' (not fourty). Talk about the link between the sounds of some of the numbers, such as six and sixty, but also listen to the exceptions. Also point out that we say, for instance, a hundred and not 'ten-ty', twenty and not 'two-ty'!

Counting in 3s, 4s, and 5s

Draw pathways by writing the missing numbers.

Steps of 3

Steps of 4

Steps of 5

If children find this difficult make a number line for them to work with or use a ruler. Encourage them to use both hands, keeping one finger on the number they are starting from and using the other hand to count. This will prevent them from counting the start number as one of the 'hops'.

Reading numbers

Join the numbers and complete the drawings.

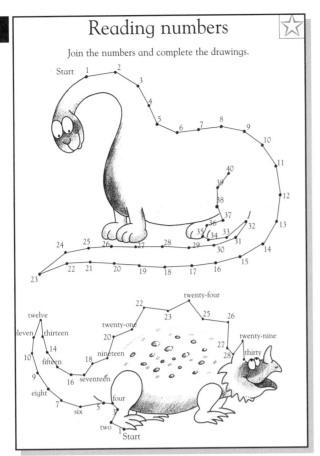

Encourage children to talk about what they see before they begin. Can they read through the numbers aloud before drawing? What would be the number before the first number or after the last one?

Tens and units

Write the tens and units.

tens — 3 tens — 30

units — 6 units — 6

30 + 6 = 36

tens — 20

units — 3

20 + 3 = 23

tens — 10

units — 7

10 + 7 = 17

tens — 30

units — 0

30 + 0 = 30

tens — 20

units — 5

20 + 5 = 25

Working with tens and units is still an important part of early mathematical understanding, and it may be that the children are used to seeing the tens and units represented vertically. Point out that it makes no difference.

Comparisons

Write more than or less than.

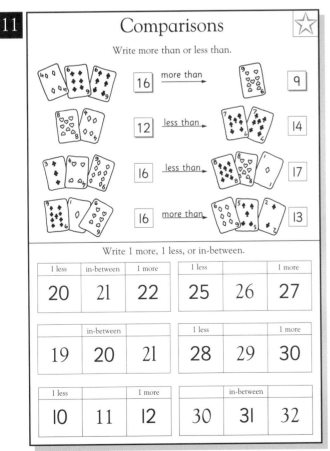

| 16 | more than → | | 9 |

| 12 | less than → | | 14 |

| 16 | less than → | | 17 |

| 16 | more than → | | 13 |

Write 1 more, 1 less, or in-between.

1 less	in-between	1 more
20	21	22

1 less		1 more
25	26	27

	in-between	
19	20	21

1 less		1 more
28	29	30

1 less		1 more
10	11	12

		in-between
30	31	32

When totalling the numbers children may use a number line (e.g. a ruler) or mental short-cuts. Number bonds, such as the pairs that make 10, are often the easiest to do. If they manage the more than/less than arrows well, you could then ask how many more or less it is.

Comparing money

Colour the one who has the most money.

Draw some coins in the purses.

Many combinations are possible but the children should ensure that the first purse has less than the tag in the middle and the second purse has more than the tag. Encourage them to use the terms 'more than', 'less than', 'in-between', 'least' and 'most'.

13 Spot the doubles ☆

Draw the missing spots and write the numbers.

3 + [3] = 6
double 3 is [6]

4 + [4] = 8
double 4 is [8]

1 + [1] = 2
double 1 is [2]

2 + [2] = 4
double 2 is [4]

6 + [6] = 12
double 6 is [12]

5 + [5] = 10
double 5 is [10]

7 + [7] = 14
double 7 is [14]

10 + [10] = 20
double 10 is [20]

Can the children relate the idea of 'doubles' to dice in board games? These are number facts that are worth learning by heart as they can then be used in mental calculations as a 'short-cut'. For example, 6+7 becomes double 6+1.

14 ☆ 10 more or less

Find 10 more than each number on the rocket.

Find 10 less than each number on the rocket.

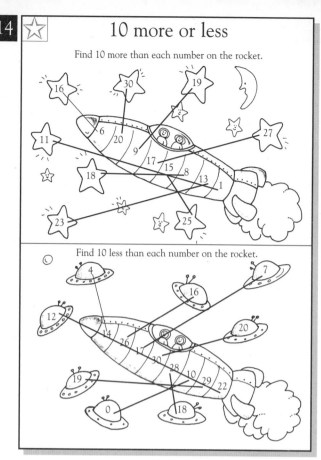

Can the children talk about what is happening to the units and tens in all cases? Can they continue some number chains for 10 more than? As with the work on doubles, familiarity with 10 more or less will help develop their mental mathematics.

15 Ordinals ☆

Colour the beads.

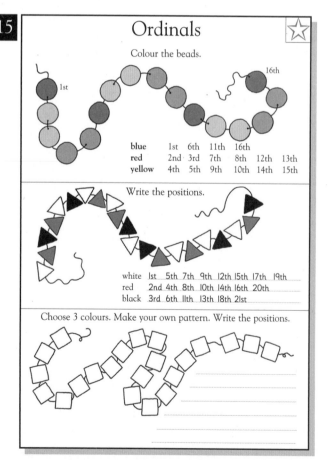

blue   1st 6th 11th 16th
red   2nd 3rd 7th 8th 12th 13th
yellow 4th 5th 9th 10th 14th 15th

Write the positions.

white   1st 5th 7th 9th 12th 15th 17th 19th
red   2nd 4th 8th 10th 14th 16th 20th
black   3rd 6th 11th 13th 18th 21st

Choose 3 colours. Make your own pattern. Write the positions.

Let the children describe the positions of each colour. Do they notice any difference in the way 1st and 21st are written, compared with 2nd and 22nd, and 3rd and 23rd? How are *most* of them written? How do they think 'thirty-first' will be written '31st', '31nd' or '31rd'?

16 ☆ Ordering

Write the numbers in order.

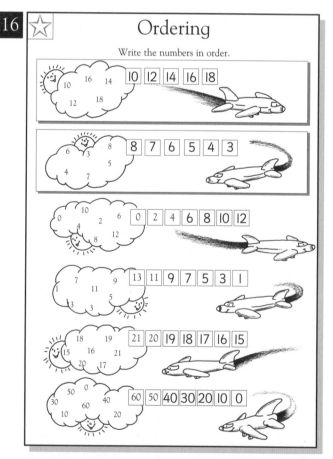

10 12 14 16 18

8 7 6 5 4 3

0 2 4 6 8 10 12

13 11 9 7 5 3 1

21 20 19 18 17 16 15

60 50 40 30 20 10 0

Do children find any of the number patterns familiar? Can they predict what the next numbers are in any of the sequences? What clues can they use to help their predictions?

17 — Halves and quarters

Colour one-half red, or one-quarter yellow.

Half or quarter?

$\frac{1}{2}$ $\frac{1}{4}$ $\frac{1}{2}$ $\frac{1}{2}$ $\frac{1}{4}$

Children may see the link between the halves and quarters and realise that two quarter pieces fit together to make a half. Practical work, with fruit etc., will help to reinforce understanding. Emphasise that each of the halves or quarters must be the same size.

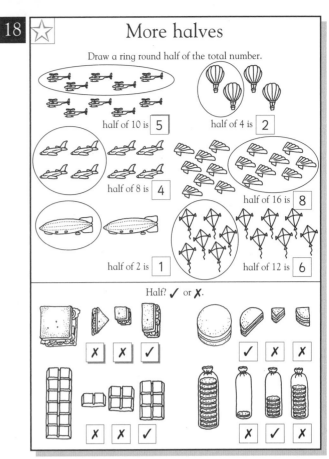

18 — More halves

Draw a ring round half of the total number.

half of 10 is 5   half of 4 is 2

half of 8 is 4   half of 16 is 8

half of 2 is 1   half of 12 is 6

Half? ✓ or ✗.

✗ ✗ ✓   ✓ ✗ ✗

✗ ✗ ✓   ✗ ✓ ✗

If children find the first section difficult, get practical objects (4 coins to represent 4 hot-air balloons) for them to handle. Splitting into halves is like sharing the objects into two equal piles. You find one-half ($\frac{1}{2}$) by counting how many there are in just one of those piles.

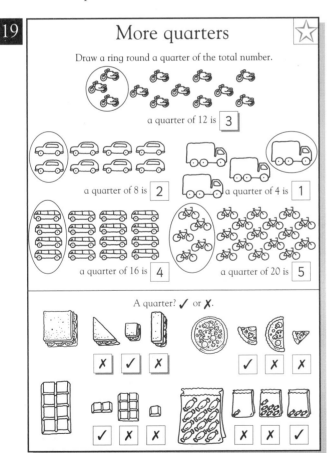

19 — More quarters

Draw a ring round a quarter of the total number.

a quarter of 12 is 3

a quarter of 8 is 2   a quarter of 4 is 1

a quarter of 16 is 4   a quarter of 20 is 5

A quarter? ✓ or ✗.

✗ ✓ ✗   ✓ ✗ ✗

✓ ✗ ✗   ✗ ✗ ✓

Finding objects for children to handle and count will enable them to tackle these activities more readily. Can they tell how many piles they will have to make to split the objects into quarters? Do they realise that they only have to count one pile to find one-quarter?

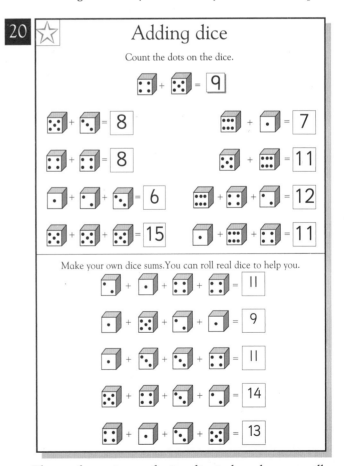

20 — Adding dice

Count the dots on the dice.

+ = 9

+ = 8   + = 7

+ = 8   + = 11

+ + = 6   + + = 12

+ + = 15   + + = 11

Make your own dice sums. You can roll real dice to help you.

+ + + = 11

+ + + = 9

+ + + = 11

+ + + = 14

+ + + = 13

Plenty of experience of using dice in board games will result in these standard patterns of spots being instantly recognisable as a number. Arranging the dots in the usual way is not as important as getting a correct total. The answers for the second section are suggestions only.

21 — Adding up

Add up the numbers on the socks.

Sock 1: 5, 6, 7 = 18
Sock 2: 3, 3, 5 = 11
Sock 3: 1, 9, 6 = 16
Sock 4: 4, 7, 2 = 13
Sock 5: 10, 3, 7 = 20

Add up the numbers on the towels.

Towel 1: 1, 4, 6, 3 = 14
Towel 2: 8, 1, 9, 4 = 22
Towel 3: 5, 5, 5, 7 = 22
Towel 4: 3, 1, 5, 7 = 16
Towel 5: 2, 4, 6, 8 = 20

Make up your own number washing.

(five blank towels with = ____)

Have the children noticed any of the number patterns? Towel 4 is the odd number and towel 5 is the even number sequence. Looking for known number facts (such as 6 and 4, 7 and 3, or 8 and 2 making 10) and doing these first, will make the whole sum much easier.

22 — Crossing out

Cross out one type of shape in each box.

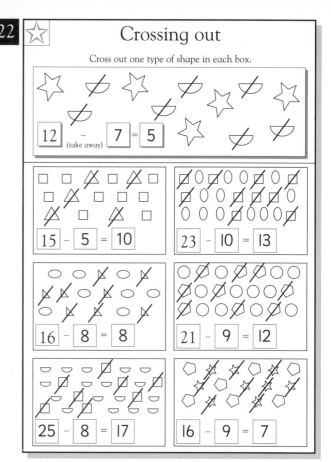

12 (take away) 7 = 5

15 − 5 = 10   23 − 10 = 13

16 − 8 = 8   21 − 9 = 12

25 − 8 = 17   16 − 9 = 7

It doesn't matter which set of shapes children choose to cross out. Point out that crossing out pictures is like 'taking away' these objects. Answers will vary if children choose to cross out the other shapes.

23 — Taking away

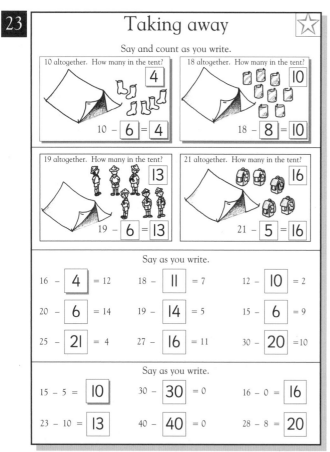

Say and count as you write.

10 altogether. How many in the tent? 4
10 − 6 = 4

18 altogether. How many in the tent? 10
18 − 8 = 10

19 altogether. How many in the tent? 13
19 − 6 = 13

21 altogether. How many in the tent? 16
21 − 5 = 16

Say as you write.

16 − 4 = 12   18 − 11 = 7   12 − 10 = 2
20 − 6 = 14   19 − 14 = 5   15 − 6 = 9
25 − 21 = 4   27 − 16 = 11   30 − 20 = 10

Say as you write.

15 − 5 = 10   30 − 30 = 0   16 − 0 = 16
23 − 10 = 13   40 − 40 = 0   28 − 8 = 20

Have children noticed the relationship between questions such as 21 − 6 = 15 and 21 − 15 = 6? Understanding links like this will greatly aid later mental calculations. Watch out for sums involving zero, which often provoke a wrong answer.

24 — Lots of

Say and count as you write.

4 + 4 + 4 = 12 legs
3 lots of 4 → 12

8 + 8 = 16 legs
2 lots of 8 → 16

5 + 5 + 5 + 5 = 20 legs
4 lots of 5 → 20

3 + 3 + 3 + 3 = 12 legs
4 lots of 3 → 12

2 + 2 + 2 = 6 legs
3 lots of 2 → 6

10 + 10 = 20 legs
2 lots of 10 → 20

When going through this work, encourage your child to talk about the pictures using the term 'lots of'. In later work, 'lots of' will be substituted by a multiplication sign and thinking of this as 'lots of' will ease the transfer.

Sharing

Share out the food.

How many each? 2

How many each? 2

How many each? 3

How many each? 4

Share out the picnic.

Encourage the use of the word 'sharing' here. Understanding will be enhanced if children can talk about what they have done by referring to the pictures. For instance, '9 bones shared between 3 dogs gives 3 bones to each dog'.

Money

Link the same amounts. Write the total.

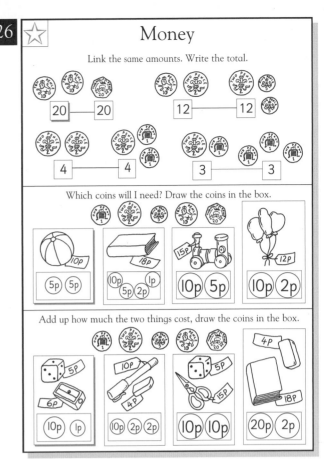

20 — 20   12 — 12

4 — 4   3 — 3

Which coins will I need? Draw the coins in the box.

5p 5p   10p 5p 1p   10p 5p   10p 2p

Add up how much the two things cost, draw the coins in the box.

10p 1p   10p 2p 2p   10p 10p   20p 2p

Discuss how using different coin combinations can make the same totals. Do children think that the best way of making 20p is by using ten two pence coins, or can they offer a better way?

How much change?

Count and say as you write.

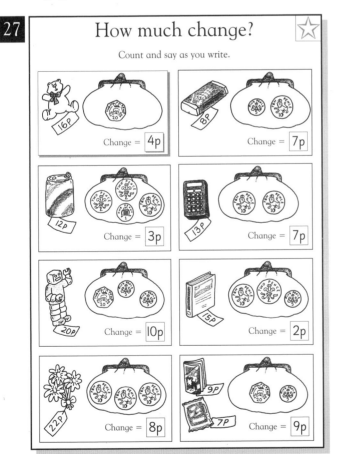

Change = 4p   Change = 7p

Change = 3p   Change = 7p

Change = 10p   Change = 2p

Change = 8p   Change = 9p

Putting the price in their head, and counting on to the amount in the purse, may be a good start for children if they do not already have a strategy. If they are still unsure, using 1p coins to count out the whole amount will make it clearer.

Days and seasons

Days of the week
Can you write them in order?

Monday Tuesday Wednesday <u>Thursday Friday Saturday Sunday</u>

Wednesday Thursday <u>Friday Saturday Sunday Monday Tuesday</u>

Saturday Sunday <u>Monday Tuesday Wednesday Thursday Friday</u>

Thursday Friday <u>Saturday Sunday Monday Tuesday Wednesday</u>

Yesterday and tomorrow

yesterday	today	tomorrow
Tuesday	Wednesday	Thursday
Sunday	Monday	Tuesday
Wednesday	Thursday	Friday
Saturday	Sunday	Monday

Seasons of the year
Draw lines to link each picture and say which season.

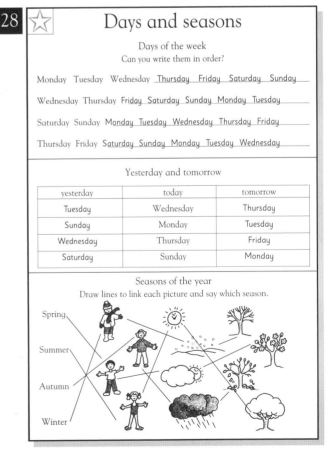

Spring

Summer

Autumn

Winter

The important point here is for children to know the order of the days and not their spellings. Tell them that each day needs a capital letter. Their reasons for linking the season pictures are important. Discuss variations; e.g., there can be snow in the spring.

Using clocks

Write the times.

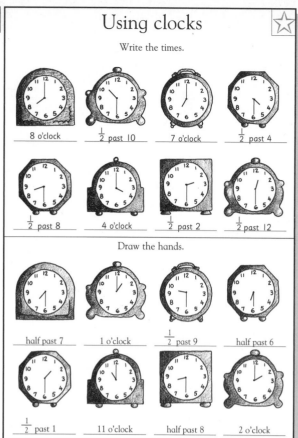

8 o'clock   ½ past 10   7 o'clock   ½ past 4

½ past 8   4 o'clock   ½ past 2   ½ past 12

Draw the hands.

half past 7   1 o'clock   ½ past 9   half past 6

½ past 1   11 o'clock   half past 8   2 o'clock

The size and correct placing of the clock hands is very important now. The children should be clear that ½ and 'half' mean the same. Relate this to their fractions work: moving from o'clock to half past creates the same shape as colouring half a round pizza.

Favourite fruits

This table shows the favourite fruits of a class of children.

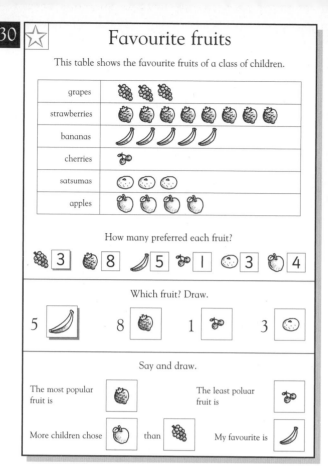

How many preferred each fruit?

🍇 3   🍓 8   🍌 5   🍒 1   🍊 3   🍎 4

Which fruit? Draw.

5 🍌   8 🍓   1 🍒   3 🍊

Say and draw.

The most popular fruit is 🍓   The least poluar fruit is 🍒

More children chose 🍎 than 🍇   My favourite is 🍌

The children should be able to give reasons for their choices. Check whether children can, with help, make up their own questions to ask you about the information shown in the pictogram.

Draw the other half

Finish the pictures

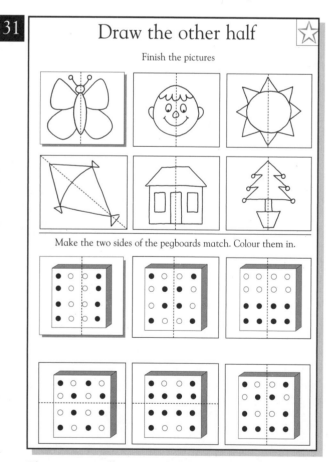

Make the two sides of the pegboards match. Colour them in.

Placing a small mirror along the line of symmetry will enable children to see the complete image. They can experiment with this before or after you ask them to draw.

Where's the bear?

on ✓ next to ✗   inside ✗ on top ✓   inside ✗ up ✓   behind ✗ beside ✓

on ✗ in ✓   in front ✓ inside ✗   under ✗ behind ✓   above ✗ under ✓

on ✓ over ✗   down ✓ up ✗

Children may need you to read some of the words to them before they can decide which one best describes the bear's position. Point out that sometimes more than one word may describe the same sort of position. For instance, 'above' can be used instead of 'on top'.

Halves and quarters

Colour one-half red, or one-quarter yellow.

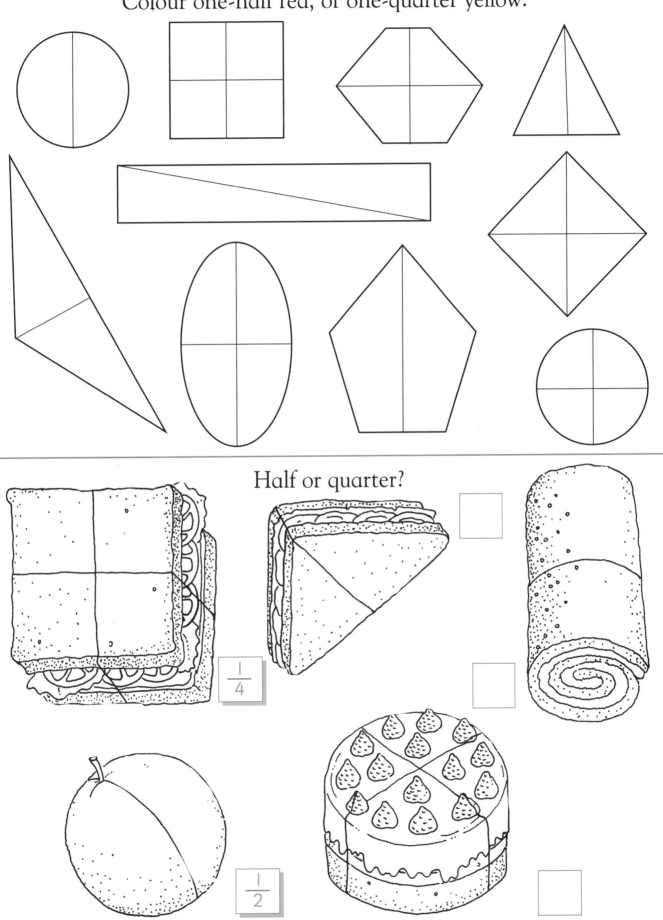

Half or quarter?

$\frac{1}{4}$

$\frac{1}{2}$

More halves

Draw a ring round half of the total number.

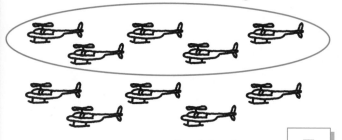

half of 10 is $\boxed{5}$

half of 4 is ☐

half of 8 is ☐

half of 16 is ☐

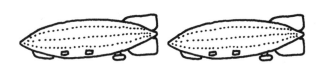

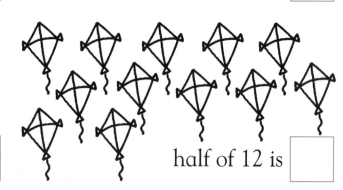

half of 2 is ☐

half of 12 is ☐

Half? ✓ or ✗.

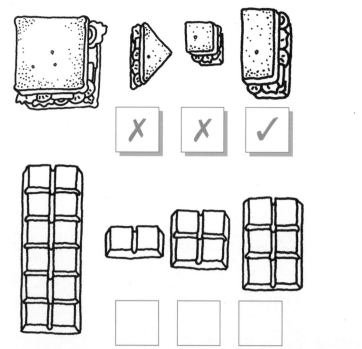

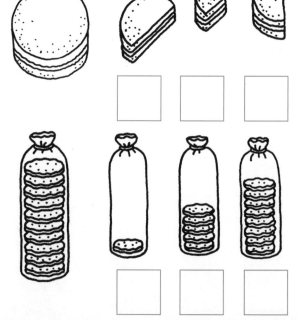

✗ ✗ ✓

More quarters

Draw a ring round a quarter of the total number.

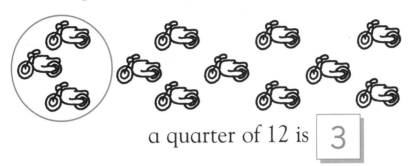

a quarter of 12 is 3

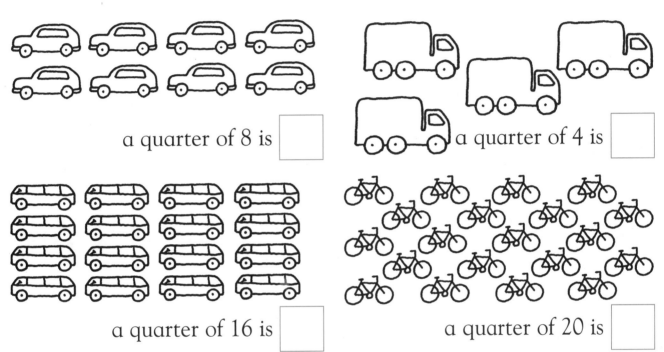

a quarter of 8 is [ ]

a quarter of 4 is [ ]

a quarter of 16 is [ ]

a quarter of 20 is [ ]

A quarter? ✔ or ✗.

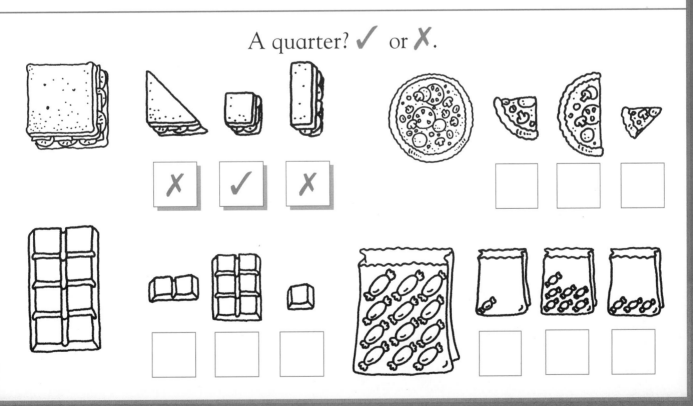

✗   ✔   ✗   [ ]   [ ]   [ ]

[ ]   [ ]   [ ]   [ ]   [ ]   [ ]

Adding dice

Count the dots on the dice.

■ + ■ = 9

■ + ■ = ☐   ■ + ■ = ☐

■ + ■ = ☐   ■ + ■ = ☐

■ + ■ + ■ = ☐   ■ + ■ + ■ = ☐

■ + ■ + ■ = ☐   ■ + ■ + ■ = ☐

Make your own dice sums. You can roll real dice to help you.

☐ + ☐ + ☐ + ☐ = ☐

☐ + ☐ + ☐ + ☐ = ☐

☐ + ☐ + ☐ + ☐ = ☐

☐ + ☐ + ☐ + ☐ = ☐

☐ + ☐ + ☐ + ☐ = ☐

Adding up

Add up the numbers on the socks.

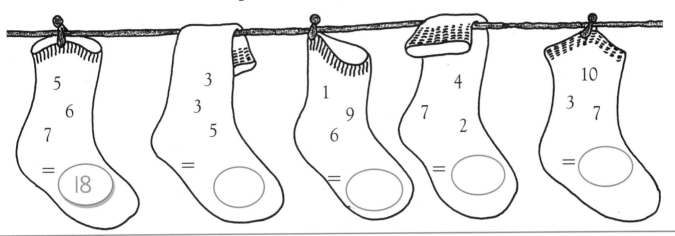

5
6
7
= 18

3
3
5
=

1
9
6
=

4
7
2
=

10
3
7
=

Add up the numbers on the towels.

1
4
6
3
= 14

8
1
9
4
=

5
5
5
7
=

1
3
5
7
=

2
4
6
8
=

Make up your own number washing.

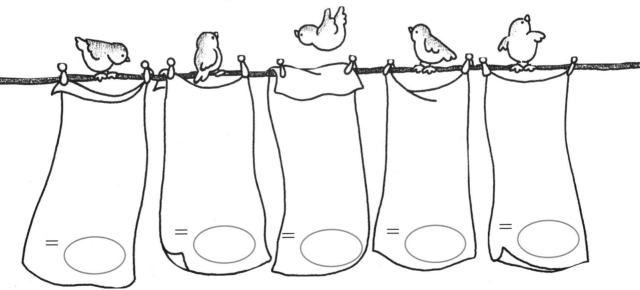

=

=

=

=

=

21

Crossing out

Cross out one type of shape in each box.

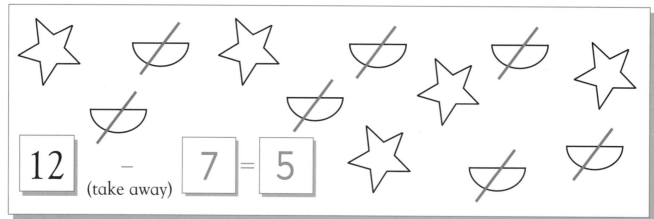

12 – 7 = 5

(take away)

15 – ☐ = ☐

23 – ☐ = ☐

16 – ☐ = ☐

21 – ☐ = ☐

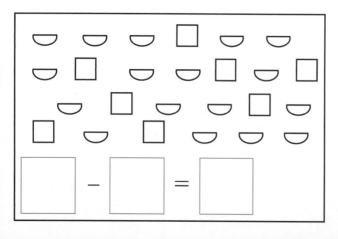

☐ – ☐ = ☐

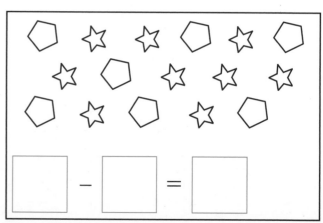

☐ – ☐ = ☐

Taking away

Say and count as you write.

10 altogether. How many in the tent?

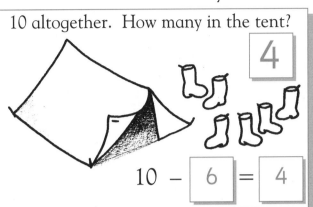

4

10 – 6 = 4

18 altogether. How many in the tent?

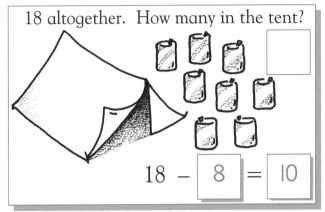

18 – 8 = 10

19 altogether. How many in the tent?

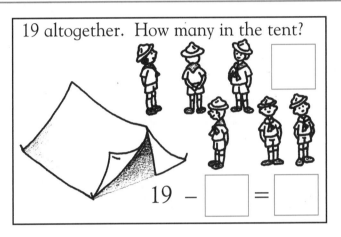

19 – ☐ = ☐

21 altogether. How many in the tent?

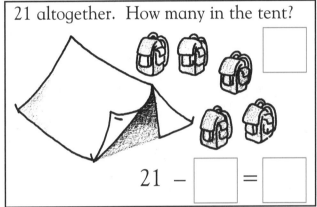

21 – ☐ = ☐

Say as you write.

16 – 4 = 12   18 – ☐ = 7   12 – ☐ = 2

20 – ☐ = 14   19 – ☐ = 5   15 – ☐ = 9

25 – ☐ = 4   27 – ☐ = 11   30 – ☐ = 10

Say as you write.

15 – 5 = 10   30 – ☐ = 0   16 – 0 = ☐

23 – 10 = ☐   40 – ☐ = 0   28 – 8 = ☐

Lots of

Say and count as you write.

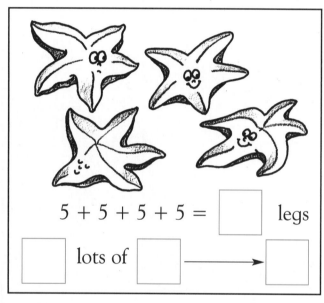

4 + 4 + 4 = $\boxed{12}$ legs

$\boxed{3}$ lots of $\boxed{4}$ ⟶ $\boxed{12}$

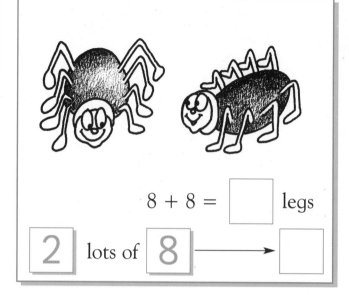

8 + 8 = $\boxed{}$ legs

$\boxed{2}$ lots of $\boxed{8}$ ⟶ $\boxed{}$

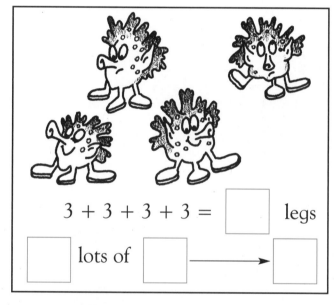

5 + 5 + 5 + 5 = $\boxed{}$ legs

$\boxed{}$ lots of $\boxed{}$ ⟶ $\boxed{}$

3 + 3 + 3 + 3 = $\boxed{}$ legs

$\boxed{}$ lots of $\boxed{}$ ⟶ $\boxed{}$

2 + 2 + 2 = $\boxed{}$ legs

$\boxed{}$ lots of $\boxed{}$ ⟶ $\boxed{}$

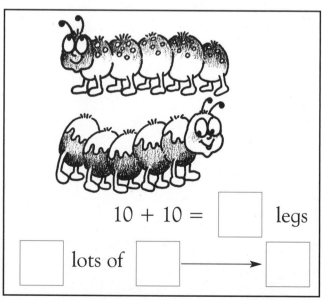

10 + 10 = $\boxed{}$ legs

$\boxed{}$ lots of $\boxed{}$ ⟶ $\boxed{}$

Sharing

Share out the food equally.

How many each? **2**

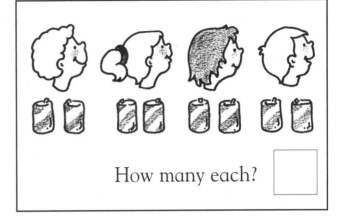

How many each?

How many each?

How many each?

Share out the picnic.

Money

Link the same amounts. Write the total.

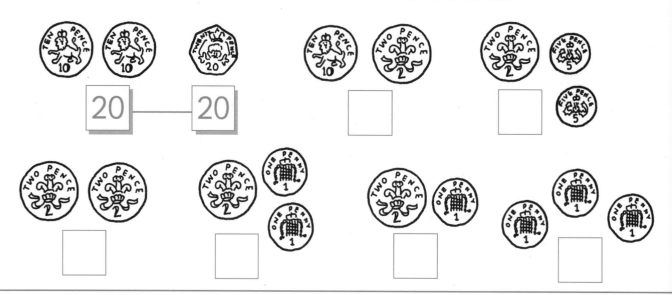

Which coins will I need? Draw the coins in the box.

Add up how much the things cost, then draw the coins in the box.

How much change?

Count and say as you write.

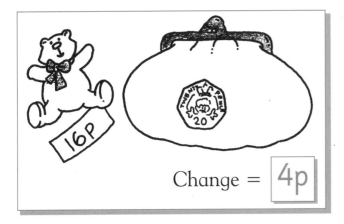

Change = 4p

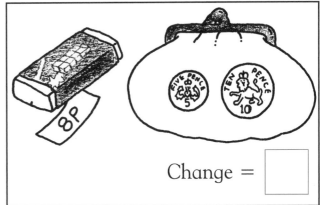

Change =

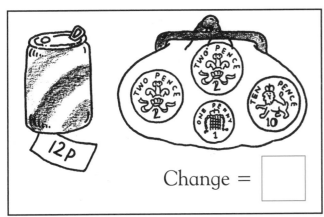

Change =

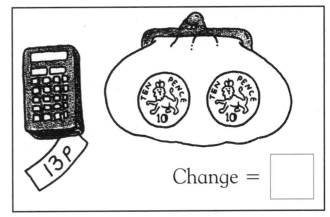

Change =

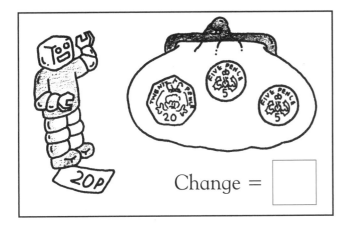

Change =

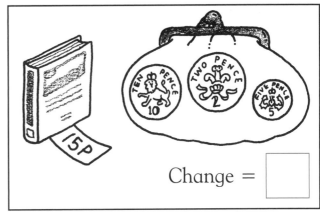

Change =

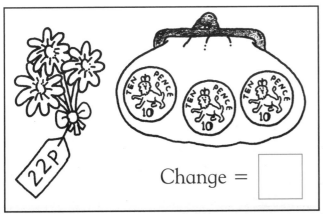

Change =

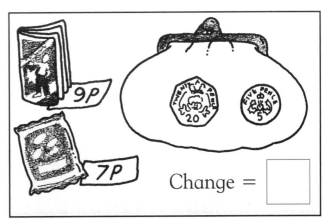

Change =

Days and seasons

Days of the week
Can you write them in order?

Monday Tuesday Wednesday <u>Thursday Friday Saturday Sunday</u>

Wednesday Thursday Fr_____

Saturday Sunday M_____

Thursday Friday S_____

Yesterday and tomorrow

yesterday	today	tomorrow
Tuesday	Wednesday	
	Monday	
	Thursday	
	Sunday	

Seasons of the year
Draw lines to link each picture and say which season.

Spring

Summer

Autumn

Winter

Using clocks

Write the times.

8 o'clock $\frac{1}{2}$ past 10

Draw the hands.

half past 7   1 o'clock $\frac{1}{2}$ past 9   half past 6

$\frac{1}{2}$ past 1   11 o'clock   half past 8   2 o'clock

Favourite fruits

This table shows the favourite fruits of a class of children.

grapes	
strawberries	
bananas	
cherries	
satsumas	
apples	

How many preferred each fruit?

Which fruit? Draw.

5 🍌   8 ☐   1 ☐   3 ☐

Say and draw.

The most popular fruit is ☐

The least popular fruit is ☐

More children chose ☐ than ☐

My favourite is ☐

Draw the other half

Finish the pictures.

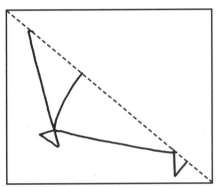  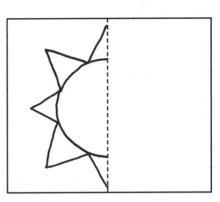

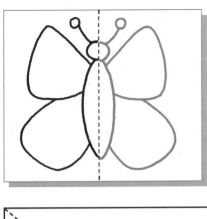 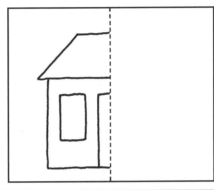 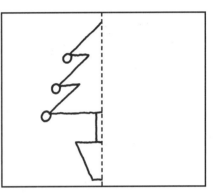

Make the two sides of the pegboards match. Colour them in.

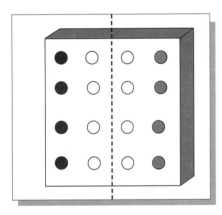 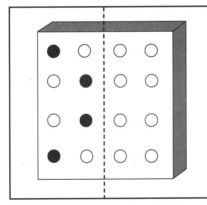 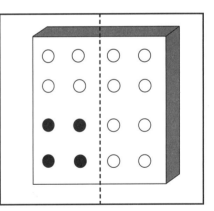

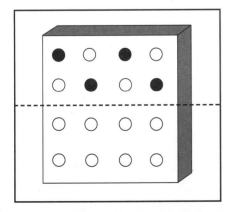 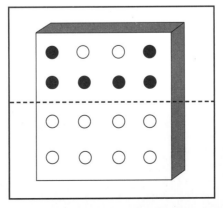 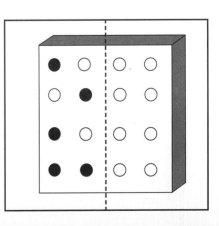

31

Where's the bear?

on ✔

next to ✘

inside ☐

on top ☐

inside ☐

up ☐

behind ☐

beside ☐

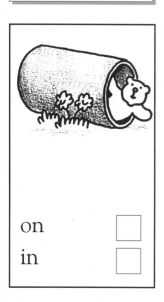

on ☐

in ☐

in front ☐

inside ☐

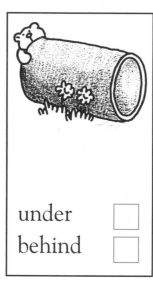

under ☐

behind ☐

above ☐

under ☐

on ☐

over ☐

down ☐

up ☐